THE
SHOSHONE

BY JOHN O'MARA

Please visit our website, www.enslow.com. For a free color catalog of all our high-quality books, call toll free 1-800-398-2504 or fax 1-877-980-4454.

Library of Congress Cataloging-in-Publication Data
Names: O'Mara, John, author.
Title: The Shoshone / John O'Mara.
Description: New York : Enslow Publishing, [2022] | Series: Native American peoples | Includes index.
Identifiers: LCCN 2020033600 (print) | LCCN 2020033601 (ebook) | ISBN 9781978521964 (library binding) | ISBN 9781978521940 (paperback) | ISBN 9781978521957 (set) | ISBN 9781978521971 (ebook)
Subjects: LCSH: Shoshoni Indians–Juvenile literature. | Shoshoni Indians–History–Juvenile literature.
Classification: LCC E99.S4 O45 2022 (print) | LCC E99.S4 (ebook) | DDC 978.004/974574–dc23
LC record available at https://lccn.loc.gov/2020033600
LC ebook record available at https://lccn.loc.gov/2020033601

Published in 2022 by
Enslow Publishing
29 E. 21st Street
New York, NY 10010

Designer: Katelyn E. Reynolds
Interior Layout: Tanya Dellaccio
Editor: Therese Shea

Photo credits: Cover, p. 1 (texture) aopsan/Shutterstock.com; cvr, pp. 1–24 (striped texture) Eky Studio/Shutterstock.com; p. 5 (left) Smith Collection/Gado/Getty Images; p. 5 (right) The New York Historical Society/Archive Photos/Getty Images; p. 6 https://upload.wikimedia.org/wikipedia/commons/2/25/Coyoteinacanoe.png; p. 7 Danita Delimont/Gallo Images/Getty Images Plus/Getty Images; p. 9 (top left) ZU_09/DigitalVision Vectors/Getty Images; p. 9 (bottom left) Grafissimo/DigitalVision Vectors/Getty Images; p. 9 (bottom right) Werner Forman/Universal Images Group/Getty Images; p. 10 ChrisBoswell/iStock/Getty Images Plus/Getty Images; pp. 11 (left), 20 Hulton Archive/Getty Images; p. 11 (right) Roman Lukiw Photography/Moment/Getty Images; p. 13 (top left) Rainer Lesniewski/iStock/Getty Images Plus/Getty Images; p. 13 (bottom left) Ted Streshinsky Photographic Archive/Corbis Historical/Getty Images; pp. 13 (bottom right), 19 (bottom), 25 (right) Historical/Corbis Historical/Getty Images; p. 15 (left) Helen H. Richardson/Denver Post/Getty Images; p. 15 (right) Otto Herschan Collection/Hulton Archive/Getty Images; p. 16 Bettmann/Getty Images; p. 17 (left) Blank Archives/Hulton Archives/Getty Images; p. 17 (right) GraphicaArtis/Archive Photos/Getty Images; p. 19 (top) UniversalImagesGroup/Getty Images; p. 21 https://upload.wikimedia.org/wikipedia/commons/f/f1/Bear_River_Massacre_1932_Monument_-_26_April_2020.jpg; p. 22 (left) Karl Gehring/Denver Post/Getty Images; pp. 22 (right), 27 Visual Studies Workshop/Archive Photos/Getty Images; p. 23 Bill Clark/CQ-Roll Call, Inc./Getty Images; p. 25 (top left) Tucker James/Shutterstock.com; p. 25 (bottom left) Courtesy of nps/gov; p. 29 (left) JASON CONNOLLY/AFP/Getty Images; p. 29 (right) MyLoupe/Universal Images Group/Getty Images.

Portions of this work were originally authored by Kristen Rajczak and published as *The Shoshone People*. All new material this edition authored by John O'Mara.

Printed in the United States of America

CPSIA compliance information: Batch #CSENS22: For further information contact Enslow Publishing, New York, New York, at 1-800-398-2504.

Find us on

CONTENTS

WORDS IN THE GLOSSARY APPEAR IN **BOLD** TYPE THE FIRST TIME THEY ARE USED IN THE TEXT.

NATIVE NATIONS

Before Europeans began exploring the Americas in the 1500s, these lands were home to **diverse** nations of Native Americans. Native peoples had long histories and **complex** ways of life. All had a deep respect for nature. They learned how to use **natural resources** to build and maintain successful communities.

The Shoshone (shoh-SHOH-nee) were one of these peoples. They lived in a large territory that is mostly today's Nevada and Idaho as well as parts of Utah, Wyoming, Montana, Oregon, and California. They were nomadic people. That means they moved around to find food.

THE SHOSHONE SOMETIMES CALL THEMSELVES NEWE OR NIMI. THESE BOTH MEAN "THE PEOPLE."

SHOSHONE NAMES

SHOSHONE (SHOH-SHOH-NEE)
SHOSHONI (SHOH-SHOH-NEE)
NEWE (NUH-WUH)
NIMI (NEE-MEE)

SHOSHONE VILLAGE

GET THE FACTS!

The name Shoshone (or Shoshoni) comes from the Shoshone word *sosoni'*. This means a kind of tall grass. Some Native Americans of the **Great Plains** called them "grass house people" because some had grass-covered homes. The Shoshone went by other names too.

ORIGIN STORIES

Stories were an important part of Shoshone **culture**. Tales tell about the beginnings of Earth and the Shoshone people. Wolf, the creator god, formed Earth with a ball of mud. Coyote, his brother, made people. They jumped from a water jug Coyote carried. This explains why different groups of Shoshone people were spread over a large area.

GET THE FACTS!

Like many Native American peoples, the Shoshone told stories featuring animals that acted like people. They passed on stories about a world of spirits too. These tales often taught the listener about why things are or how to act.

IN MANY NATIVE STORIES, THE COYOTE WAS A TRICKSTER. A TRICKSTER IS A CLEVER ANIMAL THAT OFTEN TRICKS OTHERS. IN SHOSHONE TALES, COYOTE HELPED PEOPLE TOO.

SHOSHONE STORYTELLER

Scientists know that the **ancestors** of the Shoshone and other Native Americans first settled in North America more than 12,000 years ago. Over thousands of years, different native nations settled in many places.

THE NORTHERN SHOSHONE

The Shoshone are often talked about as three groups. Each is located in a different place and shares **traditions**. They are the Northern, Eastern, and Western Shoshone.

The Northern Shoshone mostly lived near Snake River in present-day Idaho and western Wyoming. They fished for salmon and hunted bison for food and clothing. (Sometimes bison are mistakenly called buffalo.) The Northern Shoshone made cone-shaped homes, called tepees or tipis, out of bison skin. These were ideal homes for the nomadic Shoshone, because they were easy to put up and take down.

COMANCHE

GET THE FACTS!

The Comanche in present-day Texas were once Shoshone. Their ancestors were Shoshone people from the Wyoming area who traveled into the southern Great Plains. After a while, they established their own culture, different than the Northern Shoshone culture.

NORTHERN SHOSHONE
MOSTLY IDAHO, WESTERN WYOMING

LIKE ALL SHOSHONE, THE NORTHERN SHOSHONE WERE SKILLED AT FINDING FOOD, NO MATTER THE SEASON. HOWEVER, THEY SOMETIMES HAD TO MOVE TO FOLLOW OR LOCATE A FOOD SOURCE.

SHOSHONE BISON HIDE PAINTING DEPICTING HUNT

THE EASTERN SHOSHONE

The Eastern Shoshone of western Wyoming were divided into two smaller groups. They were known by the food they hunted at times. The group that lived in the valleys of Green River and Wind River was sometimes called the Buffalo Eaters. A group that lived in the Rocky Mountains, near Yellowstone Lake, was called the Sheep Eaters.

WIND RIVER LAND

THE EASTERN SHOSHONE OF WESTERN WYOMING ARE OFTEN CALLED WIND RIVER SHOSHONE.

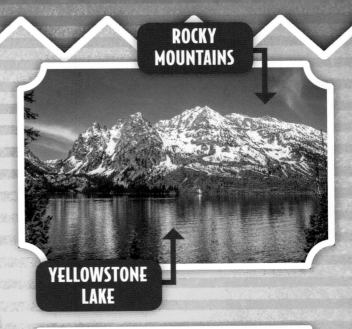

ROCKY MOUNTAINS

YELLOWSTONE LAKE

GET THE FACTS!

Europeans brought horses to America for the first time. Northern and Eastern Shoshone were likely introduced to horses around the late 1600s. Horses changed their way of life. They could get places faster, travel farther, and hunt bison more easily.

EASTERN SHOSHONE
WESTERN WYOMING

In the 1800s, the Eastern Shoshone broke into smaller bands to hunt. However, bands would gather together at times, such as in early spring in the Wind River Valley. Then they would separate again to hunt bison.

THE WESTERN SHOSHONE

The territory of the Western Shoshone was today's southern Idaho, Nevada, northwestern Utah, and Death Valley in southern California. They were sometimes called the "unmounted" Shoshone. That's because they didn't have as many horses as their relatives to the east and north.

The Western Shoshone lived in huts called wickiups, which were made of bark, branches, and grass. They hunted a little, but mostly ate food they gathered, such as seeds, berries, and nuts.

THE SHOSHONE WERE A GREAT BASIN PEOPLE. THE GREAT BASIN IS AN AREA OF THE UNITED STATES THAT DOESN'T DRAIN INTO THE OCEAN. THE GREAT BASIN PEOPLES ARE SHOWN HERE.

WESTERN SHOSHONE
NEVADA, SOUTHERN IDAHO, NORTHWESTERN UTAH, SOUTHERN CALIFORNIA

WICKIUP

GET THE FACTS!

It was likely white settlers and travelers who called the Western Shoshone "Shoshone." The Native Americans called themselves "Newe." Whites also disrespectfully called them "Diggers" because some had to dig for food since the land was poor for farming.

13

FAMILY LIFE

Even though some different Shoshone groups were far apart, they had common traditions. They traveled in small bands made up of their families, including aunts, uncles, and grandparents. A few times a year, they would all come together for celebrations or hunts.

Shoshone men hunted and, when needed, fought. Women built the family homes, cooked, and took care of children. Children gathered food and prepared for the family to move. However, they had toys and played games too. One Shoshone ball game was called shinny.

BELOW, A SHOSHONE MAN WEARS THE TRADITIONAL CLOTHING OF HIS PEOPLE. AT RIGHT, A SHOSHONE WOMAN CARRIES HER CHILD IN A CRADLEBOARD WHILE SHE WORKS.

GET THE FACTS!

The Shoshone wore clothing made from animal skins. Some were decorated with beads or porcupine quills. They also used resources such as animal bones and teeth. Later Shoshone began dressing more like Europeans. They also started to use cloth rather than animal skin.

15

A FAMOUS SHOSHONE

The first written record of the Shoshone is from 1805. That was the year an explorer named Meriwether Lewis wrote about seeing "Sosonees" (Shoshones). Lewis, William Clark, and some others were on a journey to explore the lands of the **Louisiana Purchase**.

SACAGAWEA WAS LIKELY AROUND 16 YEARS OLD WHEN SHE TRAVELED WITH LEWIS AND CLARK.

GET THE FACTS!

Sacagawea had been taken by a group of Hidatsa in 1800. Lewis and Clark met her in a Hidatsa village. On their journey together, she met her brother Cameahwait, who helped them. Below is a U.S. dollar coin, which bears Sacagawea's image.

SACAGAWEA
SAH-KAH-GAH-WEE-AH
HIDATSA FOR "BIRD WOMAN"

In a village, they met a French-Canadian trapper and his wife, Sacagawea. Sacagawea and her husband became **interpreters** on their journey. Sacagawea was a Shoshone who had been taken from her family as a girl. With Sacagawea's help, Lewis and Clark were later able to get horses from the Shoshone for their journey.

INVADERS

The fur trade brought white people to the territory of the Western Shoshone in the late 1820s. Fur trappers began killing animals on Shoshone lands. By the 1840s, gold was found around this territory too. Many settlers were coming to and through their territory trying to strike it rich.

As more white people headed west, they began claiming land on which Shoshone lived, hunted, and gathered food. Food became harder to find. As a result, some Shoshone began to steal from settlers and raid wagon trains. Fighting between whites and Shoshone increased.

THE SHOSHONE AND OTHER PLAINS PEOPLES USED BISON-SKIN SHIELDS AS WELL AS BOWS AND ARROWS. THIS PAINTING ON BISON HIDE IS FROM THE MID-1700s.

GET THE FACTS!

Shoshone were **allies** with several native peoples, such as the Crow and Paiute. They traded with them. However, they sometimes battled with others, such as the Lakota and Blackfeet of the Plains. They rarely fought to kill, however.

SHOSHONE WOMEN PREPARE AN ANIMAL HIDE FOR USE.

19

A DEADLY DAY

In the 1840s, a band of Northern Shoshone named the Northwestern Band lived in an area called the Utah Territory. They began to see more white settlers move in. At first, the two groups were friendly. However, the settlers began to use up land and resources. Fighting occurred through the 1850s and 1860s.

GET THE FACTS!

In the time leading up to the Bear River Massacre, there were fights between Native Americans and white settlers in the area. They didn't all involve the Northwestern Band of Shoshone. However, settlers didn't always see the difference between one band and another.

Shoshone Indians Salt Lake City 1869

On January 29, 1863, U.S. soldiers attacked a group of Shoshone near the modern border between Idaho and Utah. Around 350 Shoshone were killed, including many women and children. Today, this event is called the Bear River Massacre.

ONTO RESERVATIONS

As more white settlers moved west, Native Americans kept losing their historical lands. The U.S. government forced native peoples, including the Shoshone, onto lands called reservations.

WIND RIVER RESERVATION

SCHOOL ON WIND RIVER RESERVATION

GET THE FACTS!

After the Bear River Massacre, the Fort Hall Reservation was founded in 1868 in southeastern Idaho for the Shoshone and Bannock peoples. It was hard for nomadic peoples like these to change their lives to fit on a small piece of land.

THIS STATUE OF CHIEF WASHAKIE OF THE EASTERN SHOSHONE STANDS IN THE U.S. CAPITOL.

The Wind River Reservation was established in 1868 for the Eastern Shoshone. Chief Washakie, their leader, worked peacefully with the government to place the reservation on territory his people had been living on for years. However, the treaty, or agreement, Washakie signed was later **ignored**. The land promised to the Eastern Shoshone shrank. The Northern Arapaho people also live on the Wind River Reservation.

HARD TIMES

In 1875, a reservation was founded for the Lemhi Band of Northern Shoshone. It was established on their historical lands in Lemhi Valley in Idaho. After 30 years, they were forced to move. Their journey to the Fort Hall Reservation is sometimes called the Lemhi Trail of Tears.

In the 1880s, some Northern Shoshone lived among **Mormons** in Utah. By the 1960s, the Mormons decided to sell the land, called the Washakie settlement. They burned down Shoshone homes, mistakenly thinking they were empty. In 1988, Shoshone people bought back some of this land.

THE FORT HALL RESERVATION IS
LOCATED IN SOUTHEASTERN IDAHO.

THE FORT HALL RESERVATION IS
LOCATED IN SOUTHEASTERN IDAHO.

A SHOSHONE FATHER AND SON WERE
PHOTOGRAPHED IN TRADITIONAL
CLOTHING AT FORT HALL.

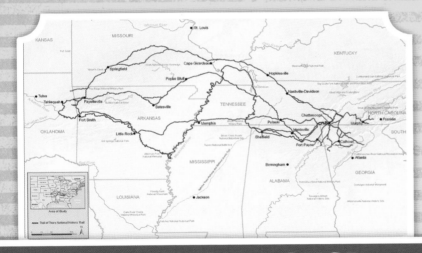

GET THE FACTS!

The first Trail of Tears was during the 1830s. Around 100,000 Eastern Woodland
Indians were forced by the U.S. government to move west. About 15,000 native
people died on the long journey. The Cherokee routes are shown above.

25

TODAY'S SHOSHONE

In 1934, the U.S. government finally allowed the Shoshone more freedom to govern themselves and live as they wanted. Around 41,000 Shoshone people live in the United States today. Many have homes on reservations, which have their own government and laws. Most don't use a chief as a leader. Instead, Shoshone vote for a group of leaders called a council.

Other Shoshone live in cities and towns across the United States. They're mainly in Idaho, Nevada, Wyoming, Montana, Utah, and California, the same lands their ancestors roamed.

A COUNCIL OF SHOSHONE AND ARAPAHO GATHER AT THE WIND RIVER RESERVATION IN THE MID-1900s.

GET THE FACTS!

Shoshone speak mainly English today. At least 2,000 still speak their native language. They learned from their parents and grandparents while growing up. However, Shoshone words can sound different depending on where the speaker lives because of the distance between Shoshone groups.

NUMBER OF SHOSHONE
41,000

NUMBER OF SHOSHONE RESERVATIONS
15

VISIT AND LEARN

Today, the Shoshone people are hard at work to keep their culture alive. On many reservations, jobs are few. Some work as ranchers or farmers. The Wind River Reservation allows companies to drill for oil and gas on their land to make money. The Fort Hall Shoshone and other Native Americans have a **casino** to raise money.

GET THE FACTS!

In the early 1900s, the Duckwater Reservation was the only Western Shoshone reservation. Many Shoshone wouldn't move from where they were living and working. The government established "colonies" where they were living. The Elko Colony, Battle Mountain Colony, and Wells Colony are three.

THE SHOSHONE HAVE OVERCOME GREAT HARDSHIPS. HOWEVER, THEY STILL CELEBRATE THEIR RICH CULTURE AND HISTORY.

Many Shoshone reservations open special events to visitors. For example, the Duckwater Shoshone Reservation in Nevada has a spring festival in June with music, dancing, and other traditions. They welcome visitors to learn about their remarkable traditions.

GLOSSARY

ally One of two or more people or groups who work together.

ancestor A relative who lived long ago.

casino A place where people play games of chance to try and win money.

complex Hard to explain or having to do with something with many parts that work together.

culture The beliefs and ways of life of a group of people.

diverse Differing from each other.

Great Plains A wide area of flat, grassy land located in the central part of North America, west of the Mississippi River and east of the Rocky Mountains.

ignore To not take notice of something on purpose.

interpreter Someone who tells the meaning of another language.

Louisiana Purchase Territory of the western United States bought from France in 1803.

Mormon A member of a Christian church founded in 1830 and centered in Salt Lake City, Utah.

natural resource Something in nature that can be used by people.

tradition A long-practiced custom.

FOR MORE INFORMATION

BOOKS

Galanis, Nika. *The Shoshoni*. New York, NY: PowerKids Press, 2018.

Lawton, Cassie M., and Raymond Bial. *The People and Culture of the Shoshone*. New York, NY: Cavendish Square, 2017.

Wilson, Wayne L. *The Shoshone*. Kennett Square, PA: Purple Toad Publishing, Inc., 2020.

WEBSITES

Shoshone Indian Culture and History
www.native-languages.org/shoshone_culture.htm
Find many links to facts about the Shoshone people.

Western Shoshone
www.californiatrailcenter.org/western-shoshone/
Read a short history of this people's history and culture.

INDEX